RESTORING STRUCTURES

Follow the Clues

by Jennifer Zeiger

CHERRY LAKE PUBLISHING · ANN ARBOR, MICHIGAN

This book is intended to introduce readers to the Next Generation Science Standards (NGSS). These standards emphasize a general set of eight practices for scientific investigation, rather than a rigid set of steps. Keywords taken from the NGSS are highlighted in the text. The eight science practices are:

1. Asking questions
2. Developing and using models
3. Planning and carrying out investigations
4. Analyzing and interpreting data
5. Using mathematics and computational thinking
6. Constructing explanations
7. Engaging in argument from evidence
8. Obtaining, evaluating, and communicating information

Published in the United States of America by Cherry Lake Publishing
Ann Arbor, Michigan
www.cherrylakepublishing.com

CONTENT ADVISER: Melissa Miller, Next Generation Science Standards Writer, Science Teacher, Farmington, Arkansas

TECHNICAL ADVISERS: Lauren Huetteman, Customer Engineer, The Boeing Company, Renton, Washington; Jacob Zeiger, Liaison Engineer, The Boeing Company, Everett, Washington

PHOTO CREDITS: tk Cover and page 1, Pajameson / tinyurl.com/n3nxkje / Public Domain; page 4, © Bizoon/Dreamstime.com; page 5, © Thiago Leite/Shutterstock.com; page 6, © aboikis/Shutterstock.com; page 7, © muratart/Shutterstock.com; page 8, © Pixel Embargo/Shutterstock.com; pages 9 and 13, © Hemis/Alamy; page 10, © Nancy Bauer/Shutterstock.com; page 11, © nikolpetr/Shutterstock.com; page 12, © Ernest R. Prim/Shutterstock.com; page 14, © ndoeljindoel/Shutterstock.com; page 15, © Andrey_Popov/Shutterstock.com; page 16, © Mr Twister/Shutterstock.com; page 17, © Graham Prentice/Shutterstock.com; page 19, © Brenda Carson/Dreamstime.com; page 20, © Khunaspix/Dreamstime.com; page 21, © Aumsama/Shutterstock.com; page 22, © AP Photo/Mike Groll; page 23, © INSADCO Photography/Alamy; page 24, © JeremyRichards/Shutterstock.com; page 25, © Hasan Shaheed/Shutterstock.com; page 26, © TTstudio/Shutterstock.com; page 27, © Dmitry Kalinovsky/Shutterstock.com; page 28, © Ineke Huizing/Dreamstime.com; page 29, © Kaspars Grinvalds/Shutterstock.com.

LIBRARY OF CONGRESS CATALOGING-IN-PUBLICATION DATA
Zeiger, Jennifer, author.
Restoring structures / By Jennifer Zeiger.
pages cm. — (Science explorer)
Summary: "Follow along with this exciting story to learn how engineers rely on scientific methods to restore aging buildings and other structures." — Provided by publisher.
Audience: Grades 4 to 6
Includes bibliographical references and index.
ISBN 978-1-63362-390-3 (lib. bdg.) — ISBN 978-1-63362-418-4 (pbk.)
— ISBN 978-1-63362-446-7 (pdf) — ISBN 978-1-63362-474-0 (ebook)
1. Architecture—Conservation and restoration—Juvenile literature.
2. Structural engineering—Juvenile literature. I. Title. II. Series: Science explorer.

NA105.Z45 2016
720.28–dc23 2015000771

Cherry Lake Publishing would like to acknowledge the work of the Partnership for 21st Century Skills.
Please visit *www.p21.org* for more information.

Printed in the United States of America, Corporate Graphics
July 2015

TABLE OF CONTENTS

CHAPTER 1

FROM OLD TO NEW

Buildings fall apart over time if no one takes care of them.

"How old do you think it is?" Sheryl asked as she stepped off the bus. A large brick house with a flat roof loomed in front of her.

Dwayne stepped down behind her. "Really old," he responded. "Look at it. It's crumbling!"

"It is not," Addy said as she joined them.

Next to them, Mo looked doubtfully at the building. "That roof doesn't seem very **stable**," he said. "Do you think it'll cave in on us?"

"That's probably why we're not going inside," Dwayne pointed out.

"Everyone line up!" called Mr. Asan. The students quietly formed a line in front of their teacher. "Does anyone remember why we're on this field trip?" he asked.

Addy raised her hand. "To look at this old house."

"Correct," Mr. Asan said. "Now why would we want to look at some old house?"

Dwayne answered, "We're learning about **structures**."

Mr. Asan smiled. "That's exactly right. Yesterday, we visited the new bridge downtown. Today, we're learning about *old* structures and how to fix them."

Some of the students noticed a woman hurrying toward them from behind the house. "Hi, Mr. Asan!" she said, shaking the teacher's hand.

Bridges are one of the many types of structures people build.

Mr. Asan thanked her for coming. Then he turned to his students. "This is Ms. Bev Freeman," he told them. "She's an **engineer**, and she's helping **renovate** this building."

"Welcome to the Taylor Home," Ms. Freeman said with a wave. "As you can see, the building needs some fixing up. Once we're finished, it will become the Taylor Theater."

"What kinds of changes will you make?" Dwayne asked.

"All sorts." Ms. Freeman paused for a moment in thought. "One of the more fun things we're doing is combining several rooms. Then we'll add a stage and some seats to make a small theater. We're also thinking of adding a small gift shop to the side, there." She pointed to an empty patch of land beside the house.

Hard work can turn an unused building into a useful space, such as a theater.

A damaged roof might collapse with little warning.

"There's another task that is more important, though. We need to make the walls and floors more stable. In fact, we can't go inside today in case something falls or collapses. It's a very old building," Ms. Freeman explained. "It was built in 1908 for the Taylor family. That's where the house gets its name. The Taylors left in 1932. A few different people have lived here since then. The building was even a community center for a while. People used the space to teach dance classes and hold meetings. However, the building has been empty for decades. Over the years, it has become unsafe."

Mo raised his hand. "What about the roof?"

"The roof is in really bad shape. We have to replace that completely," Ms. Freeman answered.

Roofs can be built in many different shapes using a wide variety of materials.

"Replace it with what?" Sheryl asked.

"That's the problem my team and I are working on now," Ms. Freeman said. "We can't agree on what kind of roof to build. Do we stick with the same type of roof the house has now? Or do we try something different?"

Mr. Asan looked excited. "That sounds like an excellent class project," he said. "What do you think, kids? Why don't we try figuring out what kind of roof is best?" Addy and Sheryl said that it was a great idea. Dwayne and a few other students cheered. Mr. Asan turned to Ms. Freeman. "Will you help us with our project?"

Ms. Freeman grinned. "I'll be happy to!"

Hal Saflieni Hypogeum was built thousands of years ago.

The Hal Saflieni Hypogeum was built on the island of Malta sometime around 4000 BCE. A hypogeum is a room or series of rooms built underground. Hal Saflieni's maze of rooms was built on three levels. Experts believe that it was used as a place of worship and for burying the bodies of people who died.

Among the most surprising aspects of the Hal Saflieni Hypogeum are its **acoustics**. On the lowest level is a chamber that people today call the Holy of Holies. The room is shaped to echo only deep sounds. A man's voice or the sound of a large drum will echo loudly off the room's walls. But higher pitched sounds, such as the sound of smaller instruments or the voices of children and women, seem to echo much less loudly and clearly.

CHAPTER 2

MAKING A PLAN

A gabled roof has two sides that meet at the top of the building.

First, Julio had a question. “What types of roofs are you thinking of using?”

“My team has designed two possible options,” explained Ms. Freeman. “As you can see, the house has a flat roof right now. The first option is to replace it with another flat roof. The second option is to build a gabled roof.”

“What’s a gabled roof?” Mo asked.

“It has two sloped sides, like the letter A.” Ms. Freeman held her arms up to form the point of a triangle. “It’s a roof shape found on a lot of houses, such as those across the street.”

"How are we going to know which kind of roof would be best?" Thea asked. "We need a plan!"

"Excellent point, Thea," said Mr. Asan. "But before we can plan our project, we should first gather information on what makes a good roof," said Mr. Asan. "Ms. Freeman, do you have the answer?"

"There are two big issues we look at when deciding on the right roof," Ms. Freeman began. "One is the cost to build it. We have to pay for all the materials the roof needs. We also pay the workers for the time and effort it takes to build it. So we ask: Is the roof affordable? Is it easy to build?

"The second issue involves figuring out how long the roof will last once it is built," she continued. "We get a lot of rain and snow around here. We need a roof that can stand up to that weather. A good, sturdy roof might

Huge amounts of snow can collect on roofs during winter storms.

need only a few repairs now and then to keep it in shape. Here, a good question is: How well does the roof hold up against bad weather?"

Mr. Asan asked, "How can we answer these questions?"

"Let's start with the first issue: the cost to build," Ms. Freeman said. "Size is a big part of cost, so our first activity should be figuring out the size of each roof option. We can also talk about factors that make a roof easier or more difficult to build."

"And the second issue?"

"For that we can build **models**. We'll use these models to test how strong or weak a roof is."

"Fantastic!" Mr. Asan declared. "Let's all do the first activity here today. We'll do the second activity in class tomorrow."

"Let's get started!" Addy said.

Some types of roofs require more frequent repairs than others.

WONDERFUL ROOFS

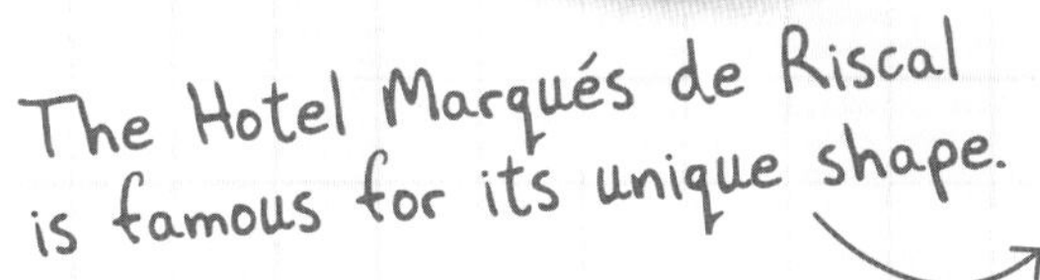

The Hotel Marqués de Riscal is famous for its unique shape.

Look at pictures of buildings around the world. You'll probably notice a lot of different roof shapes. Some are flat or gabled. Others may have several different slopes. They might even have curved shapes, such as domes or arches.

There are also roofs that take design to a new level. Some are made of unusual roofing material. In recent decades, people have begun building "green roofs." These roofs have built-in gardens of grass, flowers, or even trees. The layers of plants absorb heat, keeping the roof—and building—cooler in the summer.

Other roofs are unusual in their shape. The roof of the Leaf House outside Rio de Janeiro, Brazil, is shaped like six giant banana leaves. In Álava, Spain, the roof of the Hotel Marqués de Riscal has a complicated, ribbonlike shape. Elsewhere in Spain, the city of Barcelona boasts a number of unique roofs designed by the **architect** Antoni Gaudí. The roofs of his buildings display a range of textures. Some even include the figures of people or animals.

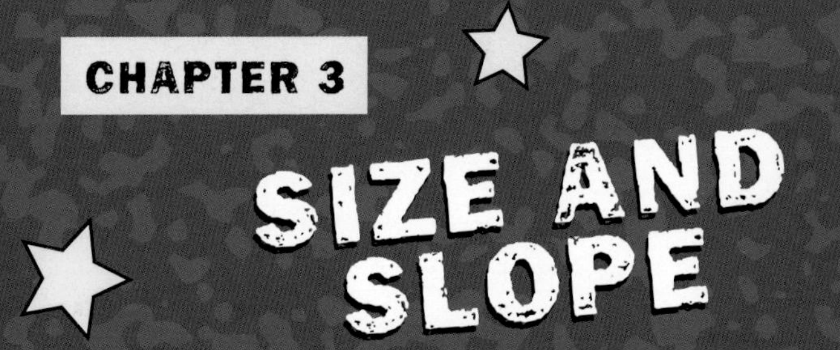

CHAPTER 3

SIZE AND SLOPE

Engineers and builders rely on careful measurements to help them plan projects.

"Our first activity is figuring out each roof's size, right?" Mr. Asan asked. Several students nodded. "Does anyone have ideas about how we might do that?"

"We could climb up and measure the roof," Dwayne suggested.

"That's one way," Ms. Freeman said. "But the roof is not stable, and it is dangerous to climb up there right now. However, there's actually a way to **estimate** a roof's size without leaving the ground."

The students looked confused. "How do you do that?" Sheryl asked.

"In two steps," Ms. Freeman said. "The first is to find how much ground sits directly underneath the roof. This is the roof's ground area. Figuring out the size of a flat roof is easy once you know the ground area. It covers the exact same amount of space that the house does. So we can simply measure around the house!" She pulled out a big tape measure. "How do you calculate area?"

Mo answered, "Multiply length times width."

"Exactly. So let's find the house's length and width." Ms. Freeman handed the tape measure to the students. Julio grabbed a notebook and pencil to write down their measurements. The measurements revealed

When taking measurements, it's always a good idea to write down results so you won't forget them.

that the house was 50 feet (15.2 meters) long. It was 40 feet (12.2 m) wide. This made the ground area 2,000 square feet (186 square meters).

Figuring out the ground area of a gabled roof required a little more work. "A flat roof doesn't stick out from the house at all," Ms. Freeman said. "But a gabled roof would. See the gabled roof on that house?" She pointed to a house across the street. "The edge of the roof sticks out past the building. It covers a larger area of ground than the house does. The gabled roof we designed would reach 1 foot (30.5 centimeters) past the house on all four sides."

"How do we measure that?" Sheryl asked.

"Why don't we have someone represent the extra foot of space?" Mo suggested. "We can place a person one foot from each side of the house. Then we can measure the distance between them."

Roofs often extend out from the sides of a building.

Some roofs have very steep pitches.

"Let's try it!" Ms. Freeman said.

This time, the area was 52 feet (15.8 m) in length. The width was 42 feet (12.8 m). Julio did some quick math in his notebook. "The gabled roof would cover 2,184 square feet," he announced.

"Or about 203 square meters," added Ms. Freeman.

"We have the ground area for both roofs now, right?" Thea asked. Ms. Freeman and Mr. Asan nodded. "So what's the second step?"

"The next step is to include the roof's **pitch**. All roofs are a little tilted, even ones that are considered flat. This is so rain will flow off the roof," Ms. Freeman said. "Engineers and architects sometimes describe pitch by saying how many inches higher the roof becomes for every 12 inches it reaches across the house." She then asked Julio if she could

borrow his notebook. When he handed it to her, she drew two diagrams on the page:

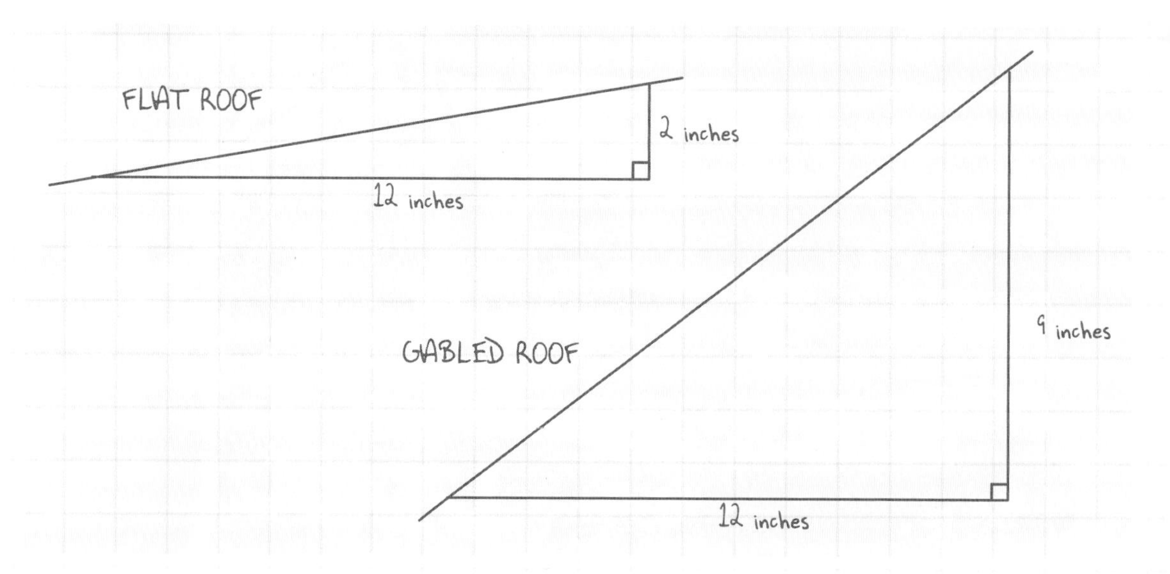

"These diagrams show the pitch for each type of roof," she explained. "A new flat roof would rise 2 inches (5 cm) for every 12 inches (30.5 cm) across. A gabled roof would rise 9 inches (23 cm). Lucky for us, engineers have come up with an easy way to figure out a roof's area using this information. We simply multiply a roof's ground area by a certain number called a multiplier. The multiplier is determined by how steep a roof's pitch is. The steeper the slope, the bigger the multiplier is. For the flat roof, we'll use 1.1 as the multiplier. For the gabled roof, we'll use 1.4. The result will give us an estimate of each roof's total area."

The class worked on the math together. They found that the area of a flat roof would be 2,200 square feet (204 sq m). The gabled roof would be about 3,058 square feet (284 sq m).

"The gabled roof is a lot bigger than the flat one," Dwayne observed. "Which means it would be more expensive to build."

"Size is just part of a roof's cost," Ms. Freeman said. "This is especially true of the gabled roof we might build. Gabled roofs can create some difficulties for roof builders. Can any of you think of what they might be?"

"The slope is dangerous to build on," Sheryl guessed. "A worker could fall off."

"That's exactly right," Ms. Freeman said. "Workers have to be careful. They might wear special harnesses to keep from falling from the roof and being hurt. The difficulty and extra equipment create extra costs."

"If we added a gabled roof, the top of the building would have to match the roof's slope, wouldn't it?" Thea asked. "Then the shape of the house would have to change, too, right?"

"That's the other big issue," Ms. Freeman answered. "Those changes would also cost money."

"So the gabled roof has to be a lot more expensive to build," Julio said.

"You're right," Ms. Freeman responded. "Be sure to remember that tomorrow when you're working on the second part of this project."

Building roofs is be dangerous work, so safety equipment is a must.

CHAPTER 4

Building a model is a great way to test out ideas before starting a project.

Ms. Freeman visited Mr. Asan's classroom the next day. The teacher broke his students up into three groups. Then they moved their desks around so each group sat clustered together.

Ms. Freeman stood up in front of the class. "Today we're going to look at roof strength. To do this, we'll build models. Models allow us to experiment with how a design works. We usually design our models and run tests using computers, but today we'll build real models to try out our ideas."

She began taking supplies out of a few boxes she had brought with her. There were bottles of glue, rolls of tape, boxes of craft sticks, packets of note cards, and three jars of pennies. Mr. Asan passed them out to the groups as Ms. Freeman talked.

"You've probably noticed that a lot of the houses around here have gabled roofs," she said. "There's a reason for that. We get a lot of rain and snow. This **precipitation** is heavy. The roof has to deal with that weight. Does anyone remember how roofs deal with rain?"

Addy raised her hand. "The roof is tilted so the rain flows off."

All roofs must be designed to deal with some precipitation.

Ms. Freeman nodded. "Rain flows off even a flat roof pretty easily, as long as it is kept in good shape. Snow is different. It collects. To make matters more difficult, the snow might not melt for months if the weather stays cold."

She continued, "You have supplies to build your models now. Let's use the craft sticks to make the walls of the house. Note cards can be used for the roof. The pennies will act as the weight of snow."

Each group made one model with a flat roof and one with a gabled roof. "Make sure you glue the roof to the house really well!" Mr. Asan told them. "And remember to give your flat roof a slight slope."

Extremely heavy snowfall can cause roofs to collapse.

A gabled roof's sloped shape makes it less likely to collapse under the weight of heavy snow.

Once the models were finished, it was time to test them. The students added a little tape to the pennies so they would stick to the roof. Then they added pennies until the roof collapsed. Each group did the test twice for each roof.

After the experiments, Ms. Freeman asked them what they had noticed. All the students agreed that the gabled roofs held several more pennies than the flat roofs in most of the tests.

Dwayne raised his hand. "So the gabled roof would probably last longer, right?"

Ms. Freeman agreed. "And it would need fewer repairs over time," she added.

DESIGNING FOR DISASTER

Stilts can keep houses out of the water in coastal areas.

Rain and snow are not the worst that weather has to offer. Natural disasters threaten people and their structures in many places around the world. To help reduce the damage these disasters can cause, people have learned to design their structures in special ways.

When a tornado occurs, the most important thing to do is find a protected place. Many homes in areas where tornadoes are common have these places built in. Storm cellars are built underground near the house. Other homes include a "safe room" inside. These rooms can withstand a tornado's strong winds and flying **debris**.

Homes where flooding is common are sometimes built on stilts. These houses can be seen along many coastal areas around the world. The stilts keep them above the floodwaters that occur during a hurricane.

Earthquakes are another problem. Engineers have developed many ways to reduce the damage they cause. One method is to add extra braces and supports. These take earthquake energy that would crack walls and floors and transfer it down into the building's **foundation**. Other additions act as shock absorbers, similar to the devices in a car that provide passengers with a smooth ride. These devices may be added below a building or to its side.

CHAPTER 5

DECIDING ON A DESIGN

Debating ideas in a group is a great way to solve problems.

"Excellent work, class," Ms. Freeman said. "We've learned a lot about our two roof designs. Now we need to figure out what this information means."

Mr. Asan asked each group to decide which roof they would choose to build and why. They discussed it for about a half hour. When they came back together as a class, each group had reached a decision. Mr. Asan turned to the first group. "Can you share with us what you decided?"

Addy cleared her throat. “We decided on the gabled roof.”

Julio was also in the group. He added, “We know it would cost more to build. However, we think the roof will be cheaper in the long run. It will need fewer repairs and will last a lot longer.”

“It also looks nicer,” Addy said. “We think this could attract more people to the theater.”

Julio smiled and nodded.

A theater's, or any other structure's, interesting appearance might make people want to visit it.

Installing a flat roof is less work than building a gabled roof.

Dwayne, Thea, and their group went next. "We decided to build the flat roof," said Dwayne. "It's cheaper to build and it worked all right for the house before."

"It didn't work that well," Julio said. "It has to be replaced now."

"We thought about that," Thea chimed in. "The flat roof is cheaper to build right now. Once the theater gets going, it will make money. Maybe by the time the roof needs to be replaced again, the theater will have plenty of money to build a gabled roof."

"Nice point," Mr. Asan said. "Now what about the third group?"

"We chose the gabled roof," Mo said.

A theater's overhanging roof might prevent people in line from needing to use umbrellas in the rain.

Sheryl explained. "Like the first group, we know the roof will be cheaper over time. But our decision also has to do with the weather. Since the gabled roof sticks out a little, it offers a bit of protection to the people lining up outside the theater."

Mo added, "A gabled roof also provides extra space in the attic to store costumes, scenery, and other objects a theater needs."

"These are great ideas," Ms. Freeman said. "Thank you so much for your help. I'll bring up all of your points with the other people working on this project. Maybe we'll finally be able to reach a decision ourselves!"

BEAUTY AND PURPOSE

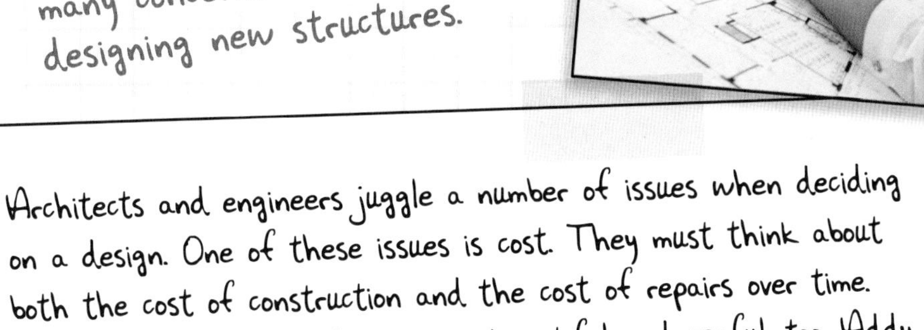

Architects must balance many concerns when designing new structures.

Architects and engineers juggle a number of issues when deciding on a design. One of these issues is cost. They must think about both the cost of construction and the cost of repairs over time.

However, the best designs are beautiful and useful, too. Addy mentioned that she liked the way a gabled roof looked. Mo pointed out that a gabled roof would provide storage space in the attic. These are ideas that architects and engineers might try to include in their decisions.

Architects and engineers face limits, though. Beauty and usefulness can cost money. Complicated designs might look nice, but they're often difficult to build. Certain extras or additions might be handy, but they might also be expensive. As a result, architects and engineers try to find a balance. An ideal design should look nice, be able to serve its purpose well, and be affordable.

GLOSSARY

acoustics (uh-KOO-stiks) the qualities of a place that affect how sound is heard in it

architect (AHR-ki-tekt) someone who designs buildings and supervises the way they are built

debris (duh-BREE) the pieces of something that has been broken or destroyed

engineer (en-juh-NEER) someone who is specially trained to design and build machines or large structures such as bridges and roads

estimate (ES-tuh-mate) to calculate something such as a value, amount, or distance in a way that is not exact

foundation (foun-DAY-shuhn) a solid structure on which a building is constructed

models (MAH-duhlz) things that someone builds as examples of something larger

pitch (PICH) the angle at which something rises

precipitation (pri-sip-i-TAY-shuhn) the falling of water from the sky in the form of rain, sleet, hail, or snow

renovate (REN-uh-vayt) modernize or restore to good condition by cleaning, repairing, or remodeling

stable (STAY-buhl) firmly fixed; not likely to fail or give way

structures (STRUHK-churz) things that have been built, such as houses, office buildings, bridges, or dams

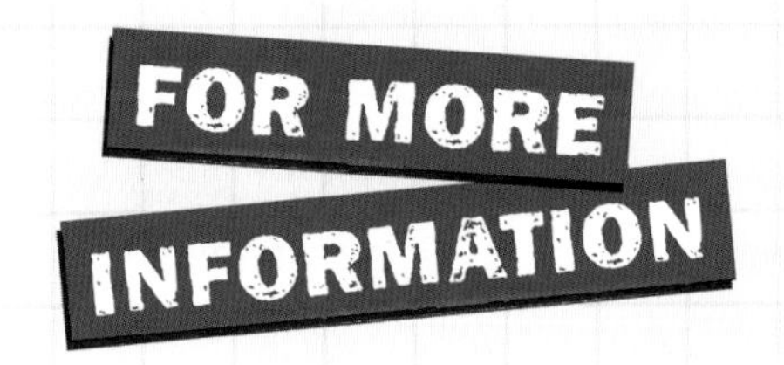

BOOKS

Brasch, Nicolas. *Triumphs of Engineering*. New York: PowerKids Press, 2013.

Paris, Stephanie. *Engineering: Feats and Failures*. Huntington Beach, CA: Teacher Created Materials, 2013.

Solway, Andrew. *Civil Engineering and the Science of Structures*. New York: Crabtree Publishing Company, 2013.

WEB SITES

National Geographic—NASA for Kids: Intro to Engineering

http://education.nationalgeographic.com/education/media/nasa-kids-intro-engineering/?ar_a=1

Visit this site to learn more about how engineers solve problems.

PBS Kids—Engineering Games

http://pbskids.org/games/engineering

Engineers are problem solvers. Check out this site to test your own problem-solving abilities with a variety of building and designing games.

INDEX

ABOUT THE AUTHOR

Jennifer Zeiger lives in Chicago, Illinois, where she writes and edits books for kids.